I am d

I am deaf

Victoria Daniell

I am deaf

## DEDICATION

This is dedicated to nannan, (my grandmother) my parents, my husband Johnny and my two amazing sons.

I am deaf

## **CONTENTS**

Acknowledgments

Introduction

I am deaf

## ACKNOWLEDGMENTS

I would like to thank my proof readers for my blog and book, Andi and Linda and to my anonymous poet.

I would also like to thank my parents, sister and my very supportive wider family including my lovely aunts and cousins (there are lots of us!) and to my mother in law Margaret for giving me ideas for the book. I would also like to thank all my friends who in one way or another have all helped me in my journey.

## INTRODUCTION

I was first diagnosed as deaf aged 3 and started to wear hearing aids around the same time.  At school I was fortunate to be in smaller classes with extra support and at home I was encouraged to use speech.  I never learned sign language until I took classes in my year out before I went to university. I have always relied on my hearing aids and lipreading to communicate. At university I gained an honours degree in History associated with English. I am married with two teenage boys. I am a support worker in a care home. So that's a bit of background about me! This book actually started life as a blog. We were going into lockdown and as a deaf person who has lipread all her life, suddenly everything seemed so difficult and challenging with the wearing of face masks. It really triggered my anxiety and I thought I would find it helpful to write about my personal experiences but at the same time try to raise some deaf awareness. As it turned out, my husband was diagnosed with cancer and there were a few other curveballs that came my way so I hope you enjoy the read.

# 1   **ZOMBIES IN A TIME OF COVID**
(June 27 2020 - at this point lockdown restrictions had started to ease)

I was born deaf - to be specific, I have bilateral congenital sensori-neural hearing loss and I wear two hearing aids. I rely a lot on lipreading and only watch programmes with subtitles. I have always grown up in the hearing world and mainly thought I could 'get away with it'. These last few months though, I've never felt 'more deaf' and I've had to confront my deafness in a different way. Instead of hiding that part of me, I feel I need to stand up and acknowledge my deafness and that it is an essential and positive part of me. I feel it's time for me to be heard. So I'm going to tell my story.

What triggered this blog was a series of issues that came up which included trying to pick up my prescription in Boots when all the staff were wearing face masks. Obviously we have been going through a period of lockdown due to Covid 19 and it has been recommended that many people wear PPE - personal protective equipment which includes face masks. Some people were wearing clear masks at the store, but the people at the prescription counter were wearing cloth ones. I explained I needed to lipread and the person concerned just leaned forward and spoke louder. I left feeling quite isolated and upset. A solution would have been to call over someone in a clear mask, but because I was upset I didn't think of that until I was safely home! I was talking to my mother about this, and she described people wearing face masks as 'zombies' and I find that to be true - there's no facial expression, you can't see if they are sad, angry or happy. You can tell so much by looking at someone's face - now they all look the same under a mask. Facial expressions really help when I lipread, too; it really gives me context to what is being said.

A few weeks ago, one of my hearing aids gave up on me. I tried everything to get it working but to no avail. Because my hearing aids work in tandem with one another, the remaining hearing aid gives a distorted sound that I've now had to get used to. Getting a new hearing aid has resulted in a lot of problems, but I'll talk about that in a future post. I was talking to a good friend this morning, and she suggested that I write a blog, as I feel I have so much to say. I had posted some comments on Facebook about my frustrations, and many people said they hadn't even thought of the issues that deaf people would have. One of my lovely friends made my husband and me clear masks that we could wear when we went out. I'll talk more about that and my hospital visit in a separate blog. Anyway, I just wanted to say a bit about myself. I'll be writing this weekly, and if you want to leave a comment please do. (but be kind!)

## 2   **THE ZOOM CALL MINEFIELD**
(July 1 2020)

As a result of Covid 19, many people have started using Zoom as a way to connect. There's something really lovely about seeing everyone's faces, isn't there? Zoom is really good in that you are focused on people's faces, and for me that means, in small numbers at least, that I can lipread. But a few issues have come up when I've been on Zoom calls, so I've come up with a few tips!

Tip #1 - Don't sit with a window directly behind you, especially if there is sunlight blazing through it - it makes your face disappear in the dark and I can't see your facial expressions or lips to read them.

Tip #2 - I really struggle with interruptions - I feel as if I need people to put their hand up when they want to speak! By the time I've located who is speaking, the conversation has moved on. I need a 'pause and rewind' button!!

Tip #3 - Obviously, the quality of the picture matters; if I can't see your lips clearly, or it's fuzzy, I will struggle. I rely a lot on facial expressions to give me a clue as to the context of the conversation. I love really expressive faces and smiley ones too!

Tip #4 - To those of you that have moustaches and beards, if you could keep on top of your grooming, that would be amazing! Many lips have been

4

hidden within a bushy beard!

Tip #5 - Think about where your head is in the shot; just half a head (usually the top half) really doesn't work for me, or sometimes there's no visual at all! I may as well give up before I've even started! I know some people feel shy about putting their faces on the screen, but if you know that one of the people you are communicating with has a hearing loss, it may be something to consider.

Tip #6 - If you need to look to the side for any reason, please do so, but only when you are not speaking!

Tip #7 - Also, keep your hands away from your face, many people don't seem to realise it, but they cover their mouth with their hands a lot - sweeping generalisation here! Also, I love it when people gesticulate with their hands, but not in front of the face please.

Tip #8 - Because of the nature of my work and volunteering, the Zoom sessions usually end in prayer. I've never really understood why people look down to the floor in prayer; shouldn't they be looking up to the heavens? I've missed out on a lot of prayers.


I have a regular Zoom call with two good friends, and I feel comfortable with them both as I know I can tell them to be quiet or to repeat themselves without feeling awkward. It's definitely a different experience for me when there are more people involved in a Zoom call, and how comfortable or appropriate it is for me to ask them to be quiet! I've put up with things like this because it's 'easier' and now I'm thinking, isn't it easier if you tell people what you need? It's difficult to say sometimes that you're struggling, especially when the other faces in the zoom call are having what looks to be a very exciting debate. Seems rude to interrupt them in mid flow, when you had lost the thread of the conversation 2 minutes ago!

I would love zoom to have subtitles - in fact everything should have subtitles. I used to imagine bubbles popping out of people's heads as they spoke so I could read their speech instead of listening to it! Also, for me, Zoom calls require a huge amount of concentration; it's similar to when I attend a conference or a meeting in which I have to take notes; I usually end up with a bad headache for quite a few hours afterwards due to the stress it takes on my body.

I hope this helps people and puts no pressure on the lucky ones who get to be on my next zoom call!

## 3   I CAN'T HEAR WITHOUT MY GLASSES
(July 8 2020)

I've made an appointment to go back to the audiology clinic to get my hearing aid sorted (I was turned away as my temperature was slightly high two weeks ago), and I spoke to someone on the phone on loudspeaker with my husband hovering in case I struggled, and she reiterated that they have to wear the PPE equipment with which they have been issued. I had a similar conversation with the audiology clinic two weeks previously. I asked how I was supposed to lipread if they all had cloth masks on, and she said she would have to take it up with her head of department. I just don't understand why no one seems to have thought of this, especially since they work in a department that helps deaf and hard of hearing people.  It should be a no-brainer, surely?

A friend visited the audiology department in Bristol and no one wore clear masks, which she struggled with, and another friend went to Pembury hospital and had to explain to her consultant why she was wearing a clear mask.

I do appreciate, though, that their hands are tied and they have to defer to the powers that be.  I've been under the care of the NHS because of my deafness for over 40 years now and they have always looked after me. Also, I'm so grateful that they have given me appointments so quickly, as it has had such a detrimental effect on me not being able to 'hear' people like I usually can. I feel it's a great shame that someone higher up hasn't had the foresight or sense to realise that face masks do not work when dealing with people who are deaf, and what a huge difference clear face masks would make. I don't want to turn a positive into a negative, but equally I don't wish to dilute the fact that it is ridiculous that they don't understand, and that no one has thought it through what a huge difference clear face masks would make!

Looking at the www.gov.uk website, 11 million people in the UK are deaf or hard of hearing. Can you imagine how many people are feeling isolated right now? A simple thing like wearing a mask has huge implications. I'm still finding it difficult to adjust to all this mask wearing; it is still very isolating and it puts extra pressure on my wonderful husband who is having to go to certain places I would have gone before lockdown. It knocks my confidence too; I'm finding that I feel anxious a lot of the time - I've stopped work zoom calls until I get my hearing aid sorted, but even then I know I'll be worrying about accessibility. I'm wondering what I'll do if I find myself in situations which warrant face masks, it's almost easier to stay at home.

Dentists wear masks all the time. When I've taken

the kids, I've explained to the dentist that I lipread and they're always very happy to lower their mask so I can understand them. My dad got a message the other day from his dentist telling them about an exciting development. You can now take photos of your mouth on your mobile phone, send them to your dentist and he will tell you what is wrong! So only people with smart phones and the dexterity to manage the technology can get seen by a dentist, who will then be wearing a mask......

- My husband is taking our cat to the vet for her annual check-up this week as we are unsure whether we have to wear masks - the chances are, the vet will, so my husband is going instead of me.

- If you get your nails done in a salon, they wear masks, but I haven't had my nails done in years so that's not a problem for me!

- My boys and husband are off to the barbers today and they have been told it's compulsory to wear masks.

- I have an appointment with my hairdresser at the end of the month but I've always sat down with them at the beginning of my appointment, explained what I wanted and then I've taken my hearing aids out and glasses off and if they need to ask me anything, they gesticulate with their hands or they wait patiently for me to pop one hearing aid back in and my glasses back on. It sounds weird but I really can't hear without my glasses! (Need to have clear vision for lipreading - mask free obviously!) I'm happiest, though, when I'm in my silent world reading a trashy mag and drinking a cup of tea while my hair is getting a pampering - it's bliss!

## 4   THE POWER OF THE WRITTEN WORD
### (July 15 2020)

I didn't utter my first sentence until I was 10.
During my teens, and when I was at secondary
school, my range of vocabulary wasn't good and I
was well behind my friends. I only really caught up
with my peers when I started at university.
There was confusion when I was little as to
whether I was deaf or had a speech, but when I
was 3 I went to Birmingham Children's hospital
who assessed me and said, according to my mum
that I was a very bright little girl, my IQ was well
above average, the problem was that I only had
one-third of the normal amount of hearing. That
was when I got hearing aids.  I don't remember
much of my childhood, but then I'm thinking that
maybe I just thought visually rather than being able
to put my thoughts into words, or maybe I made
up my own words, I'm not sure. I remember being
at school when I was about 8 and doing a
somersault over the bars and my hearing aid box
and batteries went flying but I don't remember
much else about primary school.


At around the same time, my mum spent a lot of
time with me going over the same words again and
again. I remember the Dr Seuss books, the AA
Milne books: the House at Pooh Corner, When We
Were Very young and Now We Are Six; the Ant and
Bee books and Richard Scarry. The written word

became really important to me as it allowed me to make a connection with something. Around the age of 4, I had started to read the words on people's lips and began to understand what was being said.


I remember that before I started secondary school my parents took me to London to a large bookstore and I chose my first adult books - I still remember them now – The Day of the Triffids and A Town Like Alice. I remember feeling very proud that I had grown-up books. The written word has been a huge part of my life. I remember being very confused about the words ballet and quiche. Why weren't they spoken the way they were written? I still get all my information from the written word: books, magazines, subtitles from TV/films/documentaries - it's no wonder I needed glasses from an early age! I went to an all-girls boarding school at age 11, and one reason was because they had smaller, quieter classes and they could give me more one to one attention. Also, my dad said that by that stage my language had begun to develop well and that my speech could be understood by other people. Again, I really struggle to remember much; my year out and university days are so much clearer. I enjoyed English and History and I loved Art, and I remember joining the creative writing group because the teacher made such good hot chocolate! I also remember that my history teacher told my parents that I would probably get a grade 'C' for GCSE, but if I wasn't deaf I'd probably get an 'A'.

I also remember a swimming class we had. We were working towards a swimming badge of some type and I got changed with the other girls and waited by the pool for the teacher. She then proceeded to go into a lengthy explanation about something and I had no idea what she was saying; I was waiting for her to indicate that we could go into the pool. She talked for the whole lesson and we didn't even get to swim! I went back to the changing room with the others, and then had to find the teacher once I'd got my hearing aids back in and explain that I hadn't heard a thing all lesson!

I can remember a few occasions where my peers mistook my deafness for stupidity; some would speak very slowly (which is incredibly frustrating) and some would take the mickey out of me. There were some girls who didn't actually believe I was deaf and left my hearing aids in a puddle in the swimming pool changing rooms. They just didn't understand. But, saying that, I also made some really good friends and I know they're for life.

I took a year out after leaving school and went

travelling to see a really good friend of mine in Australia. Then I went to Uni and felt like I came into my own a bit more. I met some crazy people with whom I'm still in touch today - hopefully we will make that reunion next year!

Anyway, despite being told that because I was deaf I'd only get a C at GCSE History. I ended up with a BA Honours degree in History associated with English - not too bad for someone couldn't pronounce hyperbole!

## 5   GETTING TO THE RIGHT TEMPERATURE
### (July 22 2020)

After a very long wait, I finally made it to the audiology clinic in Maidstone. I had attempted to go for an appointment 2 weeks previously but my temperature was too high. In fairness to me, it was a very hot day and I had one ear with an infection and the other was hot and sweaty having had a hearing aid in it! Anyway, I was prepared this time; we had both windows down in the car, a cool wind blew round my face and I removed my remaining hearing aid so my ear wouldn't get sweaty, but with the added bonus that I couldn't hear my husband talking... (Only joking Johnny!) We drove into the car park and I could feel my palms getting sweaty. My blood pressure was definitely rising as I walked up to the entrance and so I nonchalantly walked up to the person with the ear thermometer and offered my infection-free ear, praying the whole time while trying to look really unconcerned behind a mask. She took my temperature, scribbled it on a piece of paper and sent us through to audiology.

Honestly, I felt like jumping up and down doing star jumps yelling, yes, I'm in! But thought better of it, I didn't want to be escorted from the building once I'd got in it. Johnny and I waited at the clinic with our clear lipreading-friendly face masks on. At one point a man walked past and he seemed to stare at me a little longer than necessary and then carried on walking. I thought perhaps he had smiled at me, but how was I supposed to reciprocate if I couldn't see his face? When I mentioned it later to someone else, they pointed out that he could have been simply admiring my lipreading-friendly mask, but it was a bit disconcerting not being able to read his face. Then we were finally called in. I feel I need to say at this point that absolutely no hospital staff wore clear masks; they were all cloth ones and this is because they have to wear the masks with which they have been issued. My friendly audiologist kept his mask on throughout so luckily I had my helpful husband as a translator. I have no idea how anyone else copes, I'm so grateful that Johnny was allowed in with me. Finally, the audiologist gave me my new hearing aid and his speech seemed a little clearer, but still a bit muffled. I asked whether they had looked into getting clear masks and he said that they had, but none had managed to get approval. So I'm hoping that one day the approval will be given. I left that hospital on cloud nine, striding confidently back to the car.

I don't know how you feel, but I find a mask really difficult to navigate, especially with having hearing aids and glasses behind my ear. I've been home a few more days and I can really feel that my confidence is growing and I'm feeling less anxious about everything now my 'normal' hearing is back.

## I am deaf

Sadly I know that my anxiety will return with it becoming compulsory to wear a mask in shops, but that's another blog, and for now, I feel like a new woman!

## 6 "NO MATTER HOW SLOW YOU GO, YOU'RE STILL LAPPING EVERYONE ON THE COUCH"
(July 29 2020)

I thought I would write about exercise. All my life I've seen exercise as a chore, something to get over and done with. I've actually really struggled to enjoy it and I'm sure some of you will agree with me! Now think about the added difficulties that come from being deaf, and how much more challenging exercise is, which can make it even harder to enjoy or raise any enthusiasm to get out and do it!

I've tried various pursuits over the years. I love to swim but it makes me really anxious, as once I've taken my hearing aids and glasses off I feel very vulnerable. I can't see the clock to read the time or hear people talking. After months of thinking about it, I recently tried wild water swimming and absolutely loved it. The organisers were brilliant, going the extra mile to make it work for my needs, and this time I was prepared with my prescription goggles. They went through the course rules with me on dry land instead of in the water, and it was fantastic. Because there were hardly any people there I felt more comfortable not being able to hear than I would feel in a busy swimming pool. It was exhilarating being out in the open and I plan to go again.

I've also tried yoga and Pilates, but they always make me feel nauseous. I remember one yoga class I went to and the instructor said "close your eyes" and then she looked at me pointedly and said "close your eyes", I guess I should have told her at the beginning I needed to lipread. Anyway, it's very difficult trying to lipread doing the downward dog! Enough said.

I have also tried CrossFit and the people in my class were amazing. The instructors taking the class made sure I could see their lips move and that I understood so I couldn't get out of doing any of the difficult WODs (Workout of the Day) claiming I hadn't heard...!

I've tried classes online and on DVD but have never really got on with those; it's hard trying to exercise and read subtitles at the same time!

A couple of years ago I did a triathlon. It was very scary and way out of my comfort zone. The organisers were made aware and so I left my hearing aids with my bike and joined everyone at the pool. I couldn't hear what was going on but I'd been through the practice run so was prepared. In the pool there were signs to tell me how much further I needed to swim; then I got out of the pool and ran to my bike, popped my hearing aids and glasses on and continued. It really took me out of my comfort zone but I'm so glad I did it.

I've never felt I could completely relax with exercising and so that's why running (or jogging very slowly in my case!) has been my 'go-to' exercise. When I was growing up, my parents were marathon runners and so we ended up running together doing 5k and 10k races when I was living in Kingston. We did the Great North run together a couple of times, the Great South run, and of course, the New York marathon, the year after 9/11. I then didn't do any exercise for a long time until a friend introduced me to 'parkrun'. I've now done 70+, and while I wouldn't say I love running, I always love it afterwards! It's great getting to know the parkrun community and when we are back at parkrun, a couple of friends and I are going for the parkrun alphabet challenge - completing a parkrun beginning with every letter of the alphabet. I'm hoping to reach 100 park runs by the end of next year.

I'm signed up to do a 100k walk next May (It was postponed this year) and I'm actually really looking forward to it. I'm going on my own and I'll be walking/jogging London to Brighton. I'll be walking through the night as well and hoping to do it in about 40 hours. I may jog some of the way but we will see. This is a challenge that I really wanted to do for myself, and I know I will be able to 'relax' more. I'll be with a group of people walking through the night so I won't be totally alone but I love it when it's just me and the countryside!

That's not to say running doesn't come with its own issues; I've been in races before when people have tried to overtake (Yay, I wasn't last!) and I hadn't heard them. I did think about putting 'I am deaf' on the back of the t-shirt, particularly if I'm running on the road but I stick to pavements generally as I can't hear cars behind me. I was jogging along a lovely forest route listening to music on my headphones when I became aware of a horse rider behind me and they were shouting at me to move across; I apologised and pointed to my headphones. I play music very loudly on my headphones and sometimes I wear headphones because then people think, 'oh she can't hear' because she's listening to music and they understand. If I didn't wear headphones, then they would wonder why I've been really rude and not stepped aside. Sometimes, I've even taken my hearing aids out to just really enjoy the silence and to appreciate what's around me.

While being deaf can bring additional challenges when it comes to exercise, I don't let that get in my way. No easy excuse not to exercise because I can't hear or lip read while running, cycling or swimming: I'm not letting being deaf hold me back!

An update: I only managed 40k of my ultra 100k walk due to various reasons but I did reach my sponsorship target for a great cause, the Elizabeth Foundation for preschool deaf children. They help deaf children to learn to listen and talk. They supported my cousin and her children.

## 7   THE 'T' SWITCH
(August 5 2020)

For most of my hearing-aid wearing life, there has been an option on my hearing aid called the 't' switch. I can switch it to this setting when using the phone, over the counter in shops/banks/libraries where there is a 't' switch sign, listening to music on headphones, for the TV and places that use a loop system. A hearing loop (sometimes called an audio induction loop) is a special type of sound system for use by people with hearing aids. The loop system is something that is installed in a room or particular place which amplifies noise in that particular area and cuts out background noise and it links to my hearing aid via a magnetic field. Without the 't' switch on, if there is background music playing or someone has the radio on, that sounds just as loud as someone standing in front of me. It's very difficult sometimes to be able to differentiate between the two noises. Hearing aids are very good at amplifying background noise. The idea is that I can hear the clerks in the banks, or the woman at the reception desk or the TV better with no other noise distractions.

I used to love having the 't' switch on when I listened to the Walkman because I couldn't hear anything but the music. I had some very good school friends who, along with my sister, used to write out the lyrics of songs for me as I couldn't hear the words. If I bought a cassette or record, I would only buy the ones that had lyrics printed inside or on the cover. I used to play my favourite songs very loudly to the annoyance of my sister!

I remember I was so excited when 'closed captioning' became a thing with videos (basically subtitles). As I grew up, I remember sitting very close to the TV trying to hear what was going on, probably why I had glasses from such a young age! Now, if a programme or film doesn't have subtitles, I just don't watch it. We did have a loop system for the TV so I could cut out background noise, but that also meant I couldn't hear any conversations that were going on the room. I do enjoy going to the cinema. I usually read up about the plot beforehand so I get the gist, but I'm forever interrupting my kids/husband asking what's going on. I did use the 't' switch in the cinema once but it worked so well that I could hear what was playing on the screen next door too! Very distracting...

I also remember walking near where I lived and I had my Walkman on listening to my favourite 80s songs when I realised I'd picked up someone talking. I worked out that somehow I'd managed to pick up a vicar giving a sermon in the church opposite as I walked along the road!

I also remember at primary school that for

assembly I would wear a loop unit which consisted basically of the box style hearing aids on my chest with a collar round my neck - it looked like a really badly fitted bra! I absolutely hated wearing it as it was so obvious. Anyway, the head teacher would have to clip a similar box to her waist which was then attached to a microphone which she attached to her blouse. I remember her saying in front of the whole school - can you hear me? Meaning me. I wanted the ground to swallow me up. She called it her 'Jan Leeming' set - showing my age here!

When I first moved to London in the 90's, I had a mobile phone and I managed to find a loop system that was hearing-aid compatible with the 't' switch - it had a tiny microphone on the loop round my neck and I remember the puzzled glances I got when I could be seen talking to someone but the mobile phone was in my pocket!! They must have thought I was crazy. I've never really got on with the 't' switch for phones; I hate using the phone and will not do so unless I absolutely have to. I'm comfortable using it with family as I know their voices really well, but generally it's something I've never been comfortable with. Apparently SMS texts were originally invented as a way for deaf people to communicate, but then became popular with hearing people too. I love texting and emailing.

Unfortunately, with my new hearing aids the audiologist gave me the option of having either the 't' switch or volume control. Because the hearing aids are being made smaller, it means that the capacity to have more controls on it are gone, or so I was told. So a couple of years ago, I had to make the decision to choose one over the other - I had become so used to having both volume control and the 't' switch that it was a really difficult decision. I tried it with the 't' switch, but found it really difficult as I had to attend two conferences for work and I couldn't hear what was being said. I didn't have the capacity to turn up the volume. So I went back to the audiologist and explained that I needed the volume control instead. So I now no longer have the 't' function on my hearing aid, which makes me feel quite sad. But, saying that, it's handy to have volume control when the kids are arguing......

## 8   HOSPITALS AND SUNFLOWERS
(August 12 2020)

We have been self-isolating as my husband had an operation on Monday and so I haven't really had to deal with going into the shops and trying to communicate with people wearing masks. We have had lots of visitors to our front gate, which has been lovely, but trying to self-isolate in this hot weather (dreaming of swimming in the sea!) and then the Wi-Fi goes down for 5 days with two teenage boys in the house... It's safe to say it's been a stressful and anxious time. My husband is now on the road to recovery and will hopefully be home from hospital soon.


Today I went to visit my husband in hospital post-op and wore my clear mask. It was a very stressful experience for me and I was so anxious. Again, my temperature was too high - on account of wearing a very sweaty hearing aid in both ears. They took my temperature another two times and said it was still too high. The nurse kindly moved her mask down so I could understand what she was saying. She offered me a bottle of water to try and cool down. I got really teary again at this point because I really wanted to see my husband. I tried to fan down my ears and then she took it again. The right ear was too high and then she took my left, it was at the threshold. I could go in, 15 minutes into 1hr visiting time. I'm wondering if it's only me that has this issue, or do other hearing aid wearers have the same problem? And why can't they use forehead thermometers? Anyway, I got to the ward and a nurse gave me a new cloth mask to wear and told me to wash my hands going in. I told her I needed to lipread but she wouldn't remove her mask. I understand that people are anxious, but in an already stressful situation it really didn't feel helpful to me.

While the hospitals have to be very cautious which unfortunately makes life quite difficult for me, I've had some quite positive experiences out and about recently. Yesterday, I thought I would venture into town. I wore my clear mask with the elastic round my head otherwise I have all sorts of difficulties with getting tangled behind the ear with my hearing aids and glasses! I went to a large Tesco store very early in the morning and was pleased to see that a few of the staff were wearing clear visor masks, and the woman at the till was behind a screen and she didn't wear a mask at all. The shop itself was fairly quiet and so it was easy to adhere to social distancing. I felt safe and able to communicate if I needed to.

I also visited a furniture warehouse shop where it's very easy to socially distance. I walked inside and spoke to two good friends. They were wearing masks, but dropped them so I could 'hear' what they were saying - from a distance. It was lovely to see some friendly faces and I didn't feel so anxious. I also visited a holiday company. We had booked to go away this year but obviously had to reschedule, and I needed up to date paperwork. I knocked on the door and a representative let me in and then sat behind a screen at her desk. There were no other customers so again, I felt less anxious. She was wearing a mask, but when I explained I needed to lipread, she also took the mask off quite happily. I was able to communicate comfortably.

I also ventured to my local bank.  There was a long queue outside and I waited patiently with the others, wearing my clear mask. I was thrilled to see that the member of staff organising the queue had a clear visor on, so I was able to answer his questions with no problems.

All in all, my experience of shops/banks so far has been really positive, but I understand there's a whole other debate about the safety of not wearing a mask, but as long as it's done sensibly, adhering to social distancing, I'm happy with it. I have been thinking about buying a lanyard with a card that says that I'm hearing-impaired and need to lipread, but I'm not sure how effective that would be. I understand that if you wear a sunflower lanyard or badge it discreetly lets staff know that you have a hidden disability and you may need extra support. I wonder how many people are aware of this, and whether they do get offered support? Someone I know has worn her sunflower lanyard out and about but says that no one has offered her extra support, and in shops they seem to ignore it and don't say anything. Perhaps we need to spread the word about these lanyards so people wearing them do get the right support.

I'm visiting my husband in hospital again tomorrow, please send good vibes/thoughts/prayers my way so that I can get into the hospital with no problems. May take a fan and an ice pack with me just to be doubly sure!

## 9  NO SWEARING PLEASE
(August 19 2020)

I thought I would write about the equipment I've used as a deaf person. When I moved to London I was living in a flat, and someone from Social Services visited and established what I would need. I had a system set up in my room that whenever the smoke alarm went off, I would get an effect like sheet lightning in my room. Nothing used to wake me up but this did!! It was a really bright light that flashed intermittently until I switched it off. Luckily it didn't go off that many times, but when it did, it was usually because my flat mate got peckish at 1 or 2am in the morning and burnt the sausages! (Happened more than once!)

I also had a fantastic alarm clock. The digital clock would flash when the alarm went off, so it had to be placed fairly close to my head, and I also had a round device that I put under my pillow and it would vibrate. There were times when it fell on the floor during the night, so it wasn't entirely fail safe. I wake up naturally early so that helps too.
I remember when I was working in my first bookshop and there was a man there who used to unpack all our boxes and was also deaf. I recall asking where he was one day, and my manager told me that because he was deaf he couldn't hear his alarm and so was habitually late. I remember feeling really indignant about this.  I can't ever

remember being late for work and I felt he was making excuses. Later on when I had calmed down, I scolded myself for not having thought up that excuse for myself - I could have treated myself to a few more lie ins!

I remember trying to use the phone at work. I had a contraption that I used to strap onto the listening ear part of the phone and it was awful! If the phone rang, I had to dash to it, grab the contraption out of my pocket, try and strap it to the phone, switch that on, then switch my hearing aid on 't' and then answer the phone! Sometimes the person on the other end wondered why it was taking so long for someone to answer! I used to get so flustered and it ran on batteries too... Honestly, anyone who knows me, knows not to call me - email and text is just fine!

I also had a watch that vibrated whenever the doorbell rang or the phone rang, but I haven't worn watches in years and it has to be fairly tight to work effectively. Anyway, my kids yell at me now when the doorbell goes, and then make no move to answer it themselves! I did have a text phone which had a small screen and a keyboard on which a message could be sent via a relay typist but I lost my patience with it after about a week, waiting for a typist to become available and then waiting for them to type what the other person said - I'm not the most patient person! If I do need to speak on the phone, then I always need to use the loudspeaker option so no swearing please!

## 10  HOT WIFE...
(September 2 2020)

Should there be a second Covid wave, and I'm really hoping there won't be, please could all hospitals use a face scanner or forehead thermometer when taking a patient's temperature? My husband was in Pembury hospital for a week after an operation and, as if that was not stressful enough, I had to endure the drama of trying to get into the hospital itself! I've spoken about this briefly in a previous blog. I wear hearing aids in both ears, and on a hot day my ears can get very warm. Ear thermometers just don't work for those who have sweaty moulds in their ears!

My husband had the operation on Monday and so I was able to go along to the hospital to see him on the Tuesday. I walked in and failed the first ear thermometer test I was told to sit and try to cool myself down. It took 4 attempts of wildly trying to flap some card next to my ear, and eventually my body temperature returned to normal. I was seriously on the verge of tears.

On the second day of visiting, it took me 3 attempts to get through. I had tried shoving an ice cube down my ear in the car but had left it until I got to the hospital, which was too late, and so I had to frantically wave my hand over my ears for 5 minutes every time. Eventually, my body temperature sorted itself out. My anxiety just hit the roof!

On the third day of visiting, I decided to wrap up an ice cube round some kitchen towel and shoved it down my ear until I was almost at the entrance and I sailed through. It's so frustrating because I knew I didn't have a temperature, but it was the hottest week and I need to wear my hearing aids continually!

On the fourth day of visiting I tried a different strategy and had a mini fan.  As I approached the entrance I realised the fan had become tangled up with some of my hair, so I spent the best part of 5 minutes frantically trying to rip my hair out of the fan without anyone noticing, it then took me three attempts to get through as I had got myself into a bit of a state! Honestly, you couldn't make it up. My husband likes to say that he has the hottest wife!

On the fifth day, it 'only' took me 2 times to try and pick my husband up to take him home, by this time I never wanted to see the inside of another hospital ever again.

We went to hospital once the following week after much persuasion from my husband, and I got straight through using the ice cube trick. I then had to sit with my husband and try to 'hear' a nurse talking through her mask for 20 minutes.

My levels of stress (and don't forget not being able to get into Maidstone hospital for my audiology appointment because my temperature was too high and I had to wait 2 weeks before I could get my hearing aid fixed!) have been very high during lockdown, and it was unfortunate that Covid was rampant when my husband was in hospital. I've never visited the hospital so much in my life, and I've never felt so discriminated against. I've had such levels of anxiety and frustration and I'm really hoping I can put it all behind me. Saying that, the NHS have been absolutely wonderful to my husband and their service has been incredible.

So, please, please, use forehead thermometers if you need to do this again; I know other hospitals use them and it will save a lot of anxiety.  Please throw in some clear masks too!

## 11 I AM ENOUGH
(September 9 2020)

I remember when I was working in the bookshop and a customer came up to me and asked me a question. They had a really strong accent and I was struggling to understand them, so I asked them to repeat themselves; then a colleague came rushing over and said something along the lines of 'She's deaf, let me take over'. No doubt he thought he was doing me a favour by taking me out of the situation, but it ended up with me crying in my manager's office because I'd had that choice taken away from me and had been totally undermined by him. I know which situations are not easy for me, and I will say so and beckon a colleague over. When I was a supermarket shelf stacker in my year out many moons ago, I remember one boss who wasn't particularly nice, and I remember he told me off for something I hadn't done. I hadn't heard his request in the first place and reminded him that I was deaf. He was so shocked, no one had informed him of this earth-shattering news and I'd assumed HR had given him the heads up. He treated me with kid gloves after that like I was a piece of china! He kept out of my way as much as he could and when he had to speak to me he spoookkkeee vvveeerrryyyy ssslllooowwwlllyyyyyyy. He just didn't know how to deal with me and didn't think to ask!

# I am deaf

Whatever situation I'm in, as soon as people notice my hearing aids (and believe me, I can tell when you've noticed!) they need a second opinion about whatever I say to them. As if my opinion had now become null and void and they felt the need to check with a hearing person just in case I didn't know what I was doing. I can remember many instances when I felt like a second class citizen, and it's just through sheer ignorance. This kind of incident made me feel as if I wasn't enough as I was. It made me lose confidence in my abilities. I wondered why people couldn't look upon me as a "normal" person? (I don't like the word 'normal' anyway!) I hated that as soon as people found out I was deaf, their reaction/attitude/feelings about me changed - I felt so uncomfortable with that - I'm still the same person I was 5 minutes ago when you were talking to me... Now, I'm comfortable with people acknowledging my deafness and asking if there's anything they need to do differently. I'm also in a place now where I will just say what I need from people.

I've never understood why being deaf seemed to equate to a lack of intelligence and a lack of being a 'complete' person. Growing up, I guess I did get a feeling of not being enough at school or at a workplace, and I hated my deafness. I longed to be like the popular girls who could hear everything that was being said while I just felt inadequate, but

# I am deaf

I know that everyone is fighting their own personal battle of some sort. I tried to hide my deafness and loved it when I thought I could get away with being like a 'hearing' person. I was one of them, and therefore complete! Its only in recent years that I have felt more comfortable with my deafness; it is a part of me, it doesn't make me a lesser person. I am enough. I am a person of faith, and God made me who I am - no mistakes. It's my identity, and it makes me the person I am today.

## 12  KIDS AND VOLUME CONTROL
(September 16 2020)

Both my boys are now teenagers, but when they were born I ended up having a caesarean for both of them. I remember I had to take my glasses and hearing aids out for the operation but when they pulled the baby out, they gave me a hearing aid so I could hear them cry.

I'm so glad that my husband is such a hands-on father with the children. I remember in the early days when the boys would cry at night, I'd be sleeping soundly after taking my hearing aids out (nothing wakes me up!) and it was Johnny who woke up every time the boys started crying - sometimes he would nudge me to get out of bed and sometimes he didn't! It worked quite well as I always went to bed early and he goes to bed really late, so we had the night and morning shifts covered! Luckily the boys have pretty much slept through the night since they were 2 months old. I was able to use a baby monitor when the boys had their daytime naps, but I still kept popping to their bedroom just in case I'd missed hearing something or that the sound was off for some reason! A webcam would have been much better to use as I could have actually seen the boys on the screen to put my mind at rest.

I tried quite a few mother and baby classes, but inevitably with those, the background noise was awful and I really struggled with it. It's difficult when you go into a class with no previous information, such as who runs the class, what their names are etc. The acoustics can be awful if it's in a large hall – it's really difficult to hear as it can be quite 'echoey'. Also, I found a couple of the groups rather cliquey and didn't feel comfortable. So I never found a group that I wanted to stay with.

When the boys were toddlers, was I thankful for volume control! Sometimes I was amazed by the loud sounds that they made, so volume control was very handy in those instances. Sometimes, I was even known to switch my hearing aids off completely, which definitely helps with stress levels!
Because the doctors have no idea if my deafness is hereditary, the boys had hearing tests every year till the age of five. They have no hearing issues, though sometimes I'd beg to differ if I need their help with housework...

There were a few times that I felt quite isolated with my husband at work and two boys 17 months apart to look after. I had anxiety and used to go on long walks with them in the double buggy, and visit my grandmother who lived round the corner for a chat, and go to the park to boost my mood. I think that not being able to join in with other mums at baby groups damaged my self-esteem and I found it a struggle to join anything. My local church was very supportive though.

The boys realised from an early age that if they wanted to get my attention, they would say 'mummy, look at me'. They seemed to understand that I needed to see their faces to hear them.

I was glad when the boys started school.  You hear about parents who don't want to let their child go and are crying on the playground, but I was very happy to hand them over! It was good to get some sanity again and the boys loved their school. One thing I have passed on to my children is my love of reading.  Both boys love reading books and I think that's such an important skill to have. I particularly enjoy reading books with my hearing aids turned off, the sweet sound of silence! Getting stuck into a world of magic and imagination with no noise to interrupt me - bliss...

Now the boys are at secondary school, and its strange to think they can go into town and meet up with friends and do their own thing without needing me as much. The boys are very helpful letting me know if there's a knock on the door or if my phone is ringing and I haven't noticed! They know that I need to be able to look at their faces when they talk, yet they still shout down the stairs and I don't reply so they shout down again and I say 'what?' by which time they've had enough and come down in person to speak to me! They still haven't learned!

## 13  MY BROWN HEARING AID BOOK
(September 23 2020)

I think most of us have our few essentials that we always have with us in our handbag/backpack /designer bag and when we get a new bag, those essentials will be transferred into the new one. I have to make sure that wherever I go, I always have a supply of hearing aid batteries. And I mean, literally every time I leave the house I make sure I have my batteries on me. And you can guarantee they will run out when I'm in the middle of a really interesting conversation, or when I'm at the theatre or cinema or, like a couple of weeks ago, when I was having a lovely meal with friends! That's when I'd like a pause button while I sort my hearing aids out!

Just before lockdown started, I was so worried about not being able to get new batteries like I usually do, that I paid for quite a few packs to see me through lockdown, and they have. I usually get my hearing aid batteries courtesy of the NHS and I've never had to pay for my hearing aids or batteries, but in this instance I was concerned that during lockdown I wouldn't have access to the usual places that give out batteries.  I was worried that they would be shut and they were. They can be sent by post but that's a much slower way of doing things and I didn't know if there would be people available who would prioritise sorting out new ones and sending them back to me. Obviously, because my hearing aid broke and I had to wait for weeks for that to be sorted, I was glad I'd bought new batteries. My brown hearing aid book lists what type of batteries I need and where they are issued. It is in my rucksack along with my batteries and spare tubing etc. When they hand out the batteries, you have to produce your brown book and they enter the details.

When I go to the places that give out batteries, I always find I'm one of a kind. I feel as if I'm surrounded by elderly people and then there's me. Mind you, that's not surprising, as one of the places I can pick new batteries up from is from Age Concern. Sometimes I think, wouldn't it be lovely if I came across someone my own age and we could have a chat?

I used to be the person on the other side of the table handing out batteries; I was a hearing aid maintenance volunteer for 9 months, helping people to work out what was wrong with their hearing aid and replacing tubing and exchanging batteries. Sometimes it would be a simple thing as a small blockage in their tubing which had meant they hadn't been able to hear anyone for the past week. I discovered that a lot of people who have come to deafness much later in life sometimes find it a real struggle to get used to hearing aids. I remember a conversation I had with my great grandmother and she remarked how awful it was trying to cope with hearing loss and I came to the conclusion that it must be worse to know what it's like to have 'normal' hearing and then lose it. I've never known what it's like to have 'normal' hearing and so I've never missed it.

I think it helped that I started wearing hearing aids at such a young age, I don't remember never needing to wear them! I think I knew that they would help me. I recall not wanting to wear glasses, until I realised I needed better sight to lipread!

## 14 **LEARNING HOW TO MAKE A FUSS**
(September 30 2020)

During these interesting times, putting aside my husband's cancer diagnosis and treatment, home-schooling, too many hospital visits to mention, all the mask-wearing, temperature-taking challenges, zoom call etiquette - I thought - why not add to my stress levels and look for a new job? I currently work part time, but need to increase our income. It has occurred to me that for too long I've been hiding and not telling people I have a disability, and I have actually not been doing myself any favours. I've struggled in the past because I've not told teachers/lecturers/managers that I need to lipread because it feels like I am drawing attention to myself and I am someone who likes to blend in with the background! I remember one lecturer who faced the whiteboard for almost the whole hour and I hadn't heard a thing! I've sometimes told myself that I don't need to say anything for now, but will speak up if I need to further down the line, and then somehow I've talked myself out of it as it's terrifying to speak out in a lecture hall with a hundred other students! It goes against every fibre of my being to stand out and say to everyone, look at me! But I am different from hearing people, I am unique and there's no one like me.


My deafness is a part of who I am, and even when doing something like filling in job application forms,

# I am deaf

I've dithered over whether to put down that I have a disability. Sometimes I've ticked the box and sometimes I haven't. I personally feel it's almost too extreme to put disability - I've wondered about whether it's possible to change the wording and just put deaf. I don't see myself as 'disabled', but I am deaf. I am perfectly able. Anyway, I ticked the disabled box in this instance and explained that I needed to lipread and see people's faces.

I actually ended up applying for two jobs and had 4 interviews in total. Two with zoom and two face to face. I 'made a fuss' and I explained how to make zoom accessible to me, and therefore I felt comfortable chatting online and could see their faces clearly.
Both the face to face interviews were outside, and in that environment I was able to have a conversation without masks. They were happy to repeat something if I missed it and were aware of the noise from the road stopping our conversation while the lorry drove past!

I have to stop worrying about what other people think and I have to get rid of that mindset that I'm making too much fuss. If I'm booked to go on a training course I have to make the trainer aware of my needs, and to be honest, I still feel uncomfortable doing it. I always wonder what the other people on the course think and whether they think I'm just making a fuss. I still have to do quite a few zoom calls and will let people know from the beginning, but again, I wish I didn't have to sometimes. I'm used to hiding in the background but by doing that I've let myself down. I need to tell people so I can make my life easier and put myself more in control of the situation. I need to stand up for me.

By the way, I got the job and I can't wait to start!

## 15  A WORLD OF DIFFERENCE
(October 7 2020)

In preparation for my new job, I have been signed up to do an online course that is week-long with 9.30am - 4.30pm days. Yes, online! As a deaf person, I like to make sure that I know exactly what is happening when, how it's going to be done, who is doing it and to have as much information about the course as possible. (Of course, this also applies to social events and similar...) I received this information half an hour before it was due to start the training, through no fault of my HR dept, which flummoxed me a bit but that was ok.

The main things I was anxious about were: would I be able to see the trainer, would I see the other participants, would I have materials, power point images, would I be able to message if I couldn't hear anything and would I be able to keep up?

Anyway, as it turned out, I felt the training was very well prepared. The trainer was online the whole time so I could see her face to lipread; the only bug bear I had was that I couldn't make her picture larger to help me lipread with more ease. Some of the participants chose not to use the webcam which was fine, and some did which made it easier. Sometimes they were not clear, so my trainer, with numerous prompts from me in the private chat, repeated what they said and repeated any questions that were asked, and encouraged people to use the chat system. There was a power point on all the time, which obviously was a great help. It made the whole process much easier to follow, and I had printed out all the material in preparation. It is important for deaf people to be armed with as much info as possible, it really helps you prepare and can help with topics of conversation and give you ideas as to what people may talk about. The trainer asked questions and we could simply put down what we thought in the chat. I decided to put my webcam on and I think I must have an expressive face, as a couple of times she asked if I was ok as I looked quite confused! It's easier to get their attention with a wave if they can see me.

I did feel for the trainer as she was listening to someone ask a question and then she was repeating it and popping a quick note on the web chat for me.  She was then carrying on talking and I was messaging her at the same time, saying her picture had disappeared from the screen! Talk about a multi-tasking pro! I also sent a message to the general chat when I was trying to private message her, but it was all fine. At one point we had to watch an online video from an outside source, but there was a written transcript of the audio below the video which was very helpful. I think perhaps it would be useful to have someone who could volunteer to bullet point things that are being said off screen but I think the whole thing is such a minefield anyway!

One issue I have always had when taking part in online courses, long zoom calls, work conferences, talks and presentations that it's actually quite hard work trying to lipread and listen at the same time. If I have a break and close my eyes for 2 minutes, I've then lost the flow of the conversation so it's pretty intense. I often come away with bad headaches as I'm concentrating so much (I don't know if other lipreaders have this issue?) and I have to allow myself time to relax and have an early night to give myself a break to try and get rid of the headache.

Anyway, I came away from the training sessions I've had so far this week feeling really positive about my new job role, and I feel that the training I'm receiving has around the same quality as everyone else's, which is a huge thing for me. I'm used to missing out and not getting it all, but I did make a fuss and the trainer was informed about my needs. It's interesting when I think about it, after any sort of training that I have, I estimate how much I've managed to hear and understand, and the numbers in my head have always been around

70-90%.  But this one I feel I got about 95%, so I'm really happy. We actually covered topics such as inclusion and equality and I feel it is so important to make people aware of these issues and learn about how they can empower people. It may only mean making a small change in how you communicate with someone, or it may be including them in something they have not been a part of before; but it can make the world of difference.

## 16 **EAVESDROPPING**
(October 14 2020)

I like to think that I just go through life, happily getting on with things and then WHAM! Life hits you with something and it's so hard to stay positive. I've been having trouble with my hearing aid over the last week.  It kept getting some sort of interference - it's a loud crackling noise in your ear and it is very distracting. On Saturday morning, I tried to clean it and it was still ridiculously loud and I had to take it out. As soon as I take my hearing aid out, I feel vulnerable and I start to get upset. My hearing aids feel like such a lifeline for me and I hate that I can't control when they break. I can't remember the last time I had to get my hearing aids replaced, and then this year, of all years, both of them let me down. I never feel more deaf than I do when faced with only one hearing aid - the sound feels distorted without the other one and I really start to get very anxious.


Anyway, of course when a hearing aid breaks down, something important is usually due to happen and I had an important zoom call where I was expected to contribute. I logged on and while it was so lovely to see so many smiling faces I couldn't follow what was being said and had to switch off my video so they couldn't see me crying. I messaged the person taking the zoom call and they understood and covered for me.

# I am deaf

It's hard to explain, but I felt so frustrated at suddenly not being able to do what I've managed to do multiple times. It leaves me feeling inadequate and it makes me feel very deaf! It's still an emotion I'm not comfortable with. If I'm honest, feeling deaf makes me feel weak and vulnerable. Why can't I be like hearing people who seem to be able to hear others so effortlessly? Why do they appear to take it for granted? I'm comfortable with being deaf, but only when it doesn't inconvenience me! My morning was turned upside down because my hearing aid broke. It has that much control over how I live my life. Now I just want to hibernate again. Anyway, I have to wait 4 days for a telephone consultation with my doctor to ask him to refer me to the audiology clinic, which will probably be in Maidstone as the Tunbridge Wells clinic is probably still closed.  Then after waiting for my audiology appointment to come through, I will have to go through the whole ear thermometer/mask wearing drama again. Honestly, how my blood pressure levels are coping I'll never know.


I'll tell you one thing I do miss with all the mask wearing, is that I can no longer lipread the people walking past me in the shop or street, I haven't been on a bus, but I used to sit on the tube or train and read people's lips! It was never about anything exciting though! I used to work in an office and one of my friends sat opposite me, and whenever she had a bad day, she would simply mouth expletives always forgetting that I could lipread her. We had a good laugh about that! I suppose it's the deaf person's version of eavesdropping...

Anyway, whenever the hospital appointment arrives, I am determined to think positively and I'm sure it will no doubt go better than in the summer, with the hot weather no longer an issue for the temperature check, no need for ice cubes and no getting your hair stuck in a fan trying to cool your ear down! Fingers crossed that appointment is sooner rather than later.

## 17 **MASK ISOLATION**
(October 21 2020)

I see your eyes, but I can't read your lips.
You are telling me something,
Not a clue what that is.
I see your mask move. I know there are words.
There is information, that just can't be heard.
You speak a bit louder. What is that for?
I'm deaf I can't hear you. A fact you ignore.
I know you are trying, I will not get mad.
But 'mask isolation' is making me sad.
When will this end? When will that be?
When we all take our masks off
And I can be free.


This amazing poem was written by a lovely friend
of mine who wishes to stay anonymous. It
describes perfectly how I feel with masks. I'm
wondering how much longer we will be wearing
them or whether this is something I'm really going
to have to learn to live with long term?
I am really enjoying my new job, but masks are still
such a minefield. I attended a training course
yesterday.  All the attendees had to wear masks
but the trainer could wear a clear one. I heard all
that was going on but missed the banter and the
comments/suggestions from my colleagues. I had
nominated one of my colleagues to be my lip
speaker and he was brilliant; whenever we had to
break out into discussion groups he and I would go

outside and so we could chat. He also has a very deep voice so I could understand him better than anyone who was softly spoken. It's a way of life that I'm sure many people are struggling with. I don't want masks to be the norm. It does make it difficult to read expressions and to fully understand what people are trying to say.

The clear masks were not supposed to steam up, but they did. It made it difficult to lipread, but the trainer was very helpful and changed it for a new one when necessary and she repeated a lot of what was said by my colleagues.

It is a daily struggle. I'm still doing all this minus one hearing aid - I still don't have an audiology appointment yet. So my hearing is distorted at the moment anyway. On the plus side, though, my new colleagues have been very understanding and are keen to help out in any way they can.

## 18 **THE STRUGGLE IS REAL FOR ME**
(October 28 2020-
Second lockdown announced on 31st October)

I've just had a stressful week, due, in part, to struggling with not seeing people's faces. I know someone who isn't deaf but has also really struggled with the masks - they want to stay anonymous but are happy to share a bit of their story.

"Like Vicky I find masks very difficult but for different reasons.
Since I am on the autistic spectrum, I am exempt from wearing a mask but I feel
incredibly anxious when leaving the house.

If I do feel brave enough to venture outside, I carry around a mask and a face visor
because facing the world without a mask often takes more courage than I have.
I do wear a sunflower lanyard but many people are unaware of its meaning. Some people are very quick to judge.

Social situations now feel abnormal, awkward and scary. Talking to people who are
wearing masks is very daunting. Social communication does not come easily to me and

I am deaf

I need all the clues I can get. When people wear
masks they look quite scary, with no
facial expressions. I can't tell whether the people I
meet are happy, sad or angry.
Communication is now very much reliant on eye
contact and maintaining eye contact
can be difficult for autistic people.


The best experience I've had so far, has been with
the rail network and with the
staff at stations. They have been very
understanding and helpful. The charity
Action for Hearing Loss has worked with the
Department of Transport to help them
become aware of the needs of people who find
masks a barrier to communication.


We all want society to be as safe as possible during
this pandemic but we also need to
protect the many people who can't wear a face
mask through no fault of their own.
Perhaps the government should do more to raise
awareness of the exemptions. We
need society to have compassion and
understanding for people and their differences."


I think it is so important that we make our voices
heard, even if it is a Facebook post or an Instagram

story. So many people are finding it hard to adjust.

Just to be clear, it's not really the masks I have an issue with, it's the fact that the way how I've communicated for years has been taken away from me, and therefore every day I'm out of my comfort zone. It's like suddenly everyone has started speaking a different language!

I was actually sent home from work last week because everything had come to a head and I started crying, and when I had started I couldn't stop. It has been such hard work trying to 'hear' and having to ask people to repeat themselves over and over again and I had underestimated the stress of everything I was going through.  I just simply needed to be at home and take things easy for a couple of days. This is a real struggle, every day.

## 19 **FEELING THE LOVE**
(November 11 2020)

I've had an incredibly stressful few weeks recently including not one, but two meltdowns at work, and I still haven't got my hearing aid sorted out, and everyone is still wearing masks, and my husband is starting his second cycle of chemo, but I thought I would take a moment and focus on the positives.

This past week my husband celebrated his 50th birthday - and it really became clear to us yesterday how much love and support there is out there for us. Johnny had so many gifts and cards and we were honestly blown away by all your thoughtful gestures. We ended up with three amazing chocolate birthday cakes, messages and calls and it was so uplifting.

We bought Johnny a Lego Millennium Falcon and I was hoping it would last a few weeks, but no, the boys and him, are just doing the last pieces now! They were all together in the sitting room working on it and I just loved that! I also love how they never seem to grow out of Lego. A friend blessed us with a large storage unit so we can display all our Lego creations! We will be showing them off when we can finally have people to visit.

# I am deaf

We have had family and friends drive Johnny to hospital appointments when I've not been able to, friends have been picking up prescriptions and we have had lots of friends just simply texting to ask if we need anything. One friend went round three supermarkets looking for items on my shopping list and I was so touched by the lengths he took to do it. I have friends on 'standby' who will go shopping for us as and when we need it, and that means so much. You know who you are and we love you all!

At work, we have regular zoom calls twice a week with colleagues and they have really taken the time to understand what my needs are. The speakers look directly into the camera and the songs have subtitles! My colleagues are now wearing clear masks at work and I'm so grateful - it's made a huge difference to how I feel. I'm starting to feel a little more confident and I'm hoping that will grow. My colleagues, who I've only known a few weeks, have been brilliant and so understanding and have allowed me to take things at my own pace. When I've felt overwhelmed about lack of communication, I've been able to step back and take a break.

As we are back in lockdown, I don't have to deal with so many mask wearers and that is a blessing!! It's almost a relief that I don't have to keep going to the shops and dealing with people. We are being as careful as we can and so that means we aren't going out as much. I think this in turn means that I can give myself time to feel stronger again and to get my anxiety levels down. I'm not hiding away, I just need to give myself a break. I'm not feeling as 'deaf' as I did a few weeks ago. I am slowly finding ways of managing the masks and becoming more confident about making a fuss.

I am deaf

## 20 **DRIVING IN MY CAR**
(November 18 2020)

I experienced something completely new this week. As I am one hearing aid down, I've been having to rely a lot on my left hearing aid, and when I finished work this week, I got into my car and started to drive home. It was then, that my left hearing aid decided that there was too much moisture/wax in my ear and blocked the sound. I tried to wiggle it around a bit and then took it out in frustration, leaving me in silence. So, yes, I drove the 2 miles home in silence. In the dark. And I quite liked it! I've never been able to hear the braking point in a car, just had to rely on instinct as to when the gears needed to change and I was aware of that as I was driving. Now, please don't worry Tunbridge Wells, yes, there was a deaf driver on the loose for 2 miles but it's all perfectly safe and legal! It is legal for completely deaf people to drive, it's not like we lose our intelligence with our hearing! It's so weird, there's something quite calming about not hearing lots of noise. I use my eyes a lot more in the car as I can't rely on my hearing, so I'm pretty sure that if an ambulance had come up behind me, I'd have spotted it quicker than you would have heard it.

I actually qualify for a disabled bus pass. My hearing is deemed bad enough to qualify and yet I feel like a complete fraud. I'm physically able and my sight is fine. But I was once on the bus home late at night when I was living in London and I was sitting at the back. The bus came to a stop 30 minutes into the journey and it turned out that I had completely missed someone throwing a rock at the window and had smashed it, causing the bus driver to stop and ask everyone to get off the bus. I was very confused but understood when one of the other passengers spoke to me. I actually like to sit on the bus or train in complete silence, I find it calming and it's easier to think. Though sometimes it's not helped. I remember a lady came and sat next to me on a train and then proceeded to talk to me and I was trying to work out a way of trying to switch my hearing aids back on without her noticing. I didn't succeed!

My hearing aids can get quite sweaty in my ears, hence a breeding ground for ear infections but sometimes it feels so freeing to take them both out, such as if I'm going swimming or even on a bike ride to feel the wind in my ear, it's almost exhilarating! I do get very nervous on bikes because I can't hear anything behind me, I'd feel much safer if my bike had wing mirrors....

Anyway, my audiology appointment is this morning at my local hospital. Please send good thoughts/vibes/prayers my way because apparently they still use the in-the-ear thermometer. Thankfully, though, the days are much colder so I'm not anticipating a problem. Hopefully I'll get a new hearing aid after waiting for so long.

## 21 **MOULD COLOUR CHART**
(November 25 2020)

I went for my audiology appointment last week, and because I hadn't been wearing my hearing aid in my right ear I had already decided that the temperature check would be done in that ear. I walked into the hospital and offered the nurse that ear and went through with no problems. It did help that it was a blustery November day. I was then asked to go to the 'green zone' which was the reception area. I showed them my appointment letter and she obviously said something that I didn't hear, so she rummaged through some paperwork she had in front of her and then lifted up a laminated sign that said 'Please go to outpatients 1'. I was thrilled, it was like getting live subtitles so I thanked her and made my way to the audiology department.

I was very disappointed to see that EVERYONE was wearing cloth masks. I wonder how many of those type of laminated signs are on people's desks? The receptionist motioned at me to sit down and I watched the screen for my name to come up - at least those screens still work. The audiologist I saw was a friendly, experienced man and I explained what my issue was, that there was a loud crackling sound every time I put my hearing aid on. I put it in my ear to demonstrate and said to him that, because he's sitting right in front of me, it would probably work perfectly. To my disappointment it did! He said he would check it anyway. He heard the crackling sound for himself and said that I indeed would need a new hearing aid. I asked why he wasn't wearing a clear mask and he said there still weren't any NHS approved ones. Really? We went into lockdown in March and there are still no NHS approved ones, at all? Anywhere?

I felt like I was on a roll here and decided to air my grievances about my current hearing aids. I'd had them almost two years and both of them had needed replacing. In my very long history of wearing hearing aids, I've hardly ever needed replacements. Also, I was still very unhappy about not having the t switch function (see earlier blog) alongside the volume control function. I was told I could only have one or the other. He disagreed, he said I could go back to wearing the larger behind the ear ones and both functions would be restored. He explained that people in general like hearing aids to be invisible and therefore were happy to have a smaller one with less functions. I argued that this was not the case, I don't care about the sizing, I just need it to work for me. So he agreed that I could get brand new larger hearing aids with the functions I wanted. He created two new moulds for me (this is done by squirting a plasticine like substance into your ear to get the shape of the ear mould - a very ticklish sensation!) and when I pick up the moulds in 4 weeks' time, they will fit me with my new hearing aids. I also got a new hearing aid book and more batteries and I had a hearing test done. I was very relieved to hear that my hearing had not got worse. It's been more or less the same since my first hearing test at the age of 3.

I'm very excited about getting my new hearing aid, also because I asked if I could choose the colour of my mould. The audiologist looked through some paperwork and eventually found a colour chart for moulds! It's going to be like getting a Christmas present when I go back to the audiology clinic to pick up my brand new PINK GLITTER moulds! The anticipation!

## 22 **PARENTS EVENING**
(December 2 2020)

I really am not a fan of parents' evening - not because I'm worried what they will say about my boys, but in the way that it's been run. I feel quite intimidated but also overwhelmed, because the teachers are usually all in a hall, in my case two halls and maybe the odd room, and they are sat at desks.  We have a limited time in which we can go up and chat - it's all scheduled beforehand so there's sometimes a rush. My husband never usually finishes work on time so it's usually me who goes. And the NOISE! Imagine a hall full of parents and children and scraping chairs and people chatting.... My hearing aid does not like this! All I can hear is the background noise, and usually very little from the earnest teacher sat in front of me. I was thrilled to discover that one of my son's math's teachers had a wonderfully loud voice and was so easy to lipread - easily my favourite!! But he was the only one, I remember struggling with other teachers who were softly spoken. It doesn't help that I'm already anxious before I go and then when I bump into other parents I know, the stress of trying to hear what they are saying and worrying about missing out on some news - well, you get the gist.


Anyway, covid comes along and what happens? We have parents evening via a screen - it's like a zoom call. We have slotted times and we wait for the screen to pop up and there is the teacher, in a quiet room. We are in a quiet room. I can see their faces and what they are saying. It's just brilliant! We were stood up by one teacher, which may have been an IT blip of some sort, but otherwise it went swimmingly. I was so excited! We even had a countdown to our next appointment, I felt so much more at ease with this way of doing things. I really want them to continue doing parents evening in this way. It makes it so much more accessible to me and definitely more hearing aid friendly!

Also in the past week, I have applied for an Access to Work grant via work. We do overnights and I am not able to at the moment because I can't hear the person at the other end of the phone or the intercom, and when I'm sleeping. I need something that will wake me up should the doorbell go or the smoke alarm or the fire alarm. I can hear the fire alarm when it goes off at work, yes, it's pretty loud, but I don't know how much I'll hear if I'm in a deep sleep. Mind you, doing something like this reminds me of when the kids were tiny, you don't really sleep that well if you're listening out for sounds. I've found these watches that alert you to smoke and fire alarms - anyway, I'm really looking forward to seeing how we can navigate this! I think it'll be a learning experience for everyone. I'll keep you posted!!

## 23 **MY HEARING CAT**
(December 16 2020 – stay at home alert level on 19th
December)

I've been thinking about my cat today. She is a
lovely black and white cat and every time I open
the front door when I've been out, there she is,
waiting to greet me. She sits next to me quite a lot
(the closest I'll get to a lap cat) which is usually in
the chair next to me or because I'm usually in front
of my laptop, she will try to sit on my keyboard and
reset the font and turn my screen upside down. But
because she usually sits so close, it's useful because
if there is a knock on the door or a noise outside
she adopts her alert pose and stares intently at the
direction the noise is in. Sometimes I'll be in bed
and she will suddenly sit up and look at the
direction of the window and it makes me want to
look outside and see what has bothered her!

She is very good at waking me up in the mornings.
I don't need an alarm clock! I don't use one
anyway.. She gently nibbles at my feet or walks up
and down the bed until I get up! If she wants food
she will slink round our feet for all she is worth and
meow until she gets what she wants. She knows
how to get my attention and I think my cat is an
excellent communicator!!

I had a zoom call with Access To Work today to see

I am deaf

if they can help me with communication aids at work. I'm hoping to be able to sleep there overnight and have alert systems that will tell me if someone is ringing the house or if the smoke alarm goes off, so we will see what happens.

I'm also still waiting to hear back from the audiologist to say when I can get fitted for my new hearing aids.  I'm hoping it should be anytime now ( want those sparkly glittery pink moulds!!  I'll keep you updated.

I'm still struggling with the use of cloth masks, but I guess I'm resigned to it for now. I feel that this is my new normal and I have to learn to live with it. If there are adjustments that can be made, then I'll do it, but to be honest, I'm taking it one day at a time. I've decided that I need to give myself time to adjust to things, I've found it difficult in all areas of my life, losing that automatic access to lipreading, and I've had to mentally accept that, very begrudgingly. Sometimes I just don't feel like making a fuss when I can't hear or don't understand what's going on; I want to just get on with things and muddle through. Sometimes it feels too hard or it's too much effort to speak up, but I know I must. I get very frustrated at times and need to be able to give myself a break. At the moment it feels like there's no let-up but, I'm really

I am deaf

looking forward to the day when I can see your
lipstick colour, your moustaches and your smiles.

## 24 **PATIENCE IS A VIRTUE**
(January 6 2021)

So, I'm hoping everyone had a fairly good Christmas.  Ours was obviously quieter and we couldn't have my parents round, which was disappointing but we did have a lovely day. I've been working throughout Christmas and New Year and I think it's really helped that I no longer work from home. I'm out and getting exercise and then I can really relax when I'm home.

Anyway, I've been wondering what's been going on with my glitter moulds, so I wrote a polite email to the audiology department and this was their response:

'Thank you for your email. You should not have been advised that you would receive a fitting within 2 weeks as the mould impression has to be sent away to the manufacturers to be made. You should have been told that you would be added to a Waiting List for fitting and an appointment would be sent. The mould has now returned with a number of others and when we are in a position you will be sent an appointment for fitting.
As you will appreciate, in the current circumstances we have a reduced number of appointments due to covid restrictions and the fact we have a number of own team on sickness absence. This is difficult times and you will be sent an appointment as and

when we have one available.'

This was sent to me on 21st December. It's quite frustrating knowing they are there but I can't get an appointment. Also, Access to Work have recommended equipment for me to use at work, but they need to know the make of my new hearing aids. I did ask in the original email but they didn't reply to that question. So everything is on hold, again.

I have started something new this week and that is Slimming World! I have lost 3lb in my first 4.5 days (I joined mid-week) and I was contemplating doing the online package, but I've done that loads of times with various eating plans, so I messaged a friend who was currently doing it with groups and came to the conclusion that groups are better than trying to do it on your own. I decided to sign up, and because I'm still not confident with Zoom, I arranged to meet my 'would be' consultant Steph in her garden, it was freezing, we wore our coats, had hot water bottles and a cuppa and sat on chairs 2 metres apart! She talked through the whole process and I signed up. Obviously, there are no groups running at the moment, so it's all on Zoom! My favourite! I was a bit nervous about meeting a completely new group of people but it was ok. My consultant spoke most of the time, introducing us to it all, and I know her well so I'm used to her voice. My consultant is going to try and get subtitles on Zoom for next week's meeting, so we will see how that goes!  Wish me luck with my weight loss....

## 25 **MY SUPERPOWER**
(January 20 2021)

Not much has happened over the past couple of weeks except that I survived a 7 day shift at work - it went surprisingly quickly! The equipment I was going to get to help me at work hasn't arrived yet and I'm still waiting for an appointment with the audiology clinic. I guess things will start moving again when lock-down is over and then I will finally get my glitter moulds and my super-duper new equipment.

Some good news though, I got my half stone loss sticker today and I was slimmer of the week 2nd week running! Feeling very encouraged by my progress and long may it continue. I'm finding I have to prepare and plan things a lot more, but it's really helped.

Also, the Zoom calls I have with Slimming World now have subtitles! Thank you Steph! Yes, zoom has subtitles but you have to pay for them. I feel it's my way of being able to communicate with others effectively but should people have to pay so I can understand? It doesn't make sense to me. If I join a Zoom call, then the only way I can get subtitles is if the host pays for them; they're not free. I don't understand the logic. I just can't get my head round it. Why should others have to pay to enable me to communicate better? Unless there's a way round it or someone knows differently? I'd love to know.

The equipment that I will get for work will help me when doing nights and hopefully will enable me to be able to communicate via the entry phone and the house phone. Through my care work, though, I have come to realise that listening is such a huge part of what I do, and being deaf doesn't stop you being a good listener. You can read body language, the way people hold themselves, the way they move. I've always been able to 'recognise' people from afar, not from their faces but by the way they move/walk - long before I can make out their features. You can read their faces (not as well as we used to before face masks), but eyes still say a lot as does the way they dress or take care of themselves. Sometimes you listen for the things that aren't being said. Also, it does help that in a few situations I can still lipread, so I can see what people are muttering under their breath!

A good friend last week made me realise that lipreading is in fact a superpower: I can do something most people around me can't. Just call me wonder woman!

## 26 **BRAVER THAN I'VE EVER BEEN**
(February 3 2021)

I've been thinking a lot this past weekend as I have been in a reflective mood. It's almost a year since we first went into lock-down and this year has been our most challenging yet as a family. Before the first lock down, we had no health worries, I forgot I was deaf and my boys were getting exercise walking to school and meeting their friends. 10 months later, we have got through a cancer diagnosis (Johnny got the all clear last week), I started a new job, the boys are stuck at home all day home-schooling and I've never felt more deaf.

Up until Covid, I think I was hiding how I really felt about my deafness and I think a part of me was embarrassed by it. Covid has forced me to show everyone who I really am and the journey has been terrifying. I've had to complain, make a fuss, admit I can't hear, I'm still waiting for my glitter moulds, I've struggled on zoom calls instead of face to face (I'm one hearing aid down again....) and I have to explain to strangers why I can't understand them. I'm the sort of person who likes to hide in the background, but I've really had to start sticking up for myself more, trying not to be embarrassed or apologetic when I've had to explain. It has felt quite isolating. I think it would have really helped me if I knew someone who had a similar hearing loss to my own and what their experience has been. It's a strange feeling thinking that you're the only one who knows what it is like, but I have been really encouraged by other people who have come forward to tell me that they have hearing issues too.

Dare I say it, but out of all this, even though I still get frustrated and angry, I think I'm coming out of my shell and feeling a little more confident as time goes by. I think my faith has played a huge part in accepting myself more, especially in the past year. And I do have a superpower! I can't forget I'm deaf while everyone is wearing masks and so I've had to really face that part of myself that I've always tried to ignore. But I think I'm getting to a place where I feel more comfortable being me, and writing the blog has been quite a cathartic process. I feel vulnerable yet stronger than I've ever been. I feel braver than I did at the beginning.

On a separate note, guess who won slimmer of the week award twice? Since I started on 1st January, I've now lost 9lb. I think a new me may be starting to emerge!

## 27 **BIONIC WOMAN**
(October 2021)

It's been quite a few months since I last wrote, so here is an update. I am now doing overnights at work, thanks to the equipment from Access to Work. I have had the equipment fully installed which enables me to be alerted when the fire alarm goes off, when someone is at the front door or the phone rings. I have a pager on my person which vibrates to alert me. I also have it attached to the bed under my pillow on overnights – this is to ensure it doesn't fall on the floor. I have a new 'magic' pen which helps me to hear my colleagues in the masks better. It's used like a microphone and I can point it at them or they can hold it when something important needs to be said. At one point it worked so well that when I left the room I could hear my two colleagues saying that they hoped it would work for me so I went running back into the office and repeated what they had said – it was so funny to see the look on their faces like they had been caught out!

There was one frustrating moment when someone came round to finally fix the fire alarm pager system; we had been waiting weeks and he had literally a ten minute window. We asked if he had done a lateral flow test and he hadn't, and he didn't have time to do one on the premises, so we had to wait another two weeks!

# I am deaf

I have done quite a lot of training for my job and I attended a training session via Zoom which unfortunately went really badly. The webcam of the presenter froze, no one else could use their webcams and she hadn't seen my messages that I had sent her privately. Needless to say, I didn't put up with it and I left. They rescheduled, and the next training session couldn't have gone better. The trainer kept checking in with me. She asked that where possible, could people please use webcams, and encouraged people to use the chat too.

We also had a training session that was all day face-to-face and I loved the trainer. His father was deaf and so he was a really good lip speaker, and he knew about my magic pen as his father uses one – he made sure I didn't miss out on anything. It really makes such a difference when people understand your needs.

Anyway, as I said, I'm doing overnights and I can't help but give myself a pat on the back for that – I feel really proud of myself for being able to do what others perhaps take for granted.

I did pick up my glitter moulds from the audiology clinic eventually and I love them! I asked if they had clear masks, and she said yes, and swapped her cloth one for a clear one. I wondered why I even had to ask her to do that in an audiology clinic of all places. Why not ensure that everyone there wears a clear mask, because there may be people who feel uncomfortable asking them to change from a cloth one.? There's a photo on the back of the book if you want to take a look!

## 28 THE MENOPAUSE
(October 2021)

Another thing that has transpired during covid is the realization that I am peri-menopausal. Hence the crying at work, my mood swings (Johnny will tell you!) the palpitations and night sweats, levels of anxiety were through the roof, the feeling that I might have dementia or I was actually going mad (forgot to put my seatbelt on and realized when I was almost halfway to my destination – that has never happened before!), the cramps, you name it. I spoke to my doctor about the possibility of looking into HRT, and before looking into it further she sent me off for a scan and blood tests which revealed a shadow on my uterine lining. I was told that it could be a polyp or, worst case scenario, cancer. So here I was, just gone through covid, and my husband's cancer diagnosis, working in a place where my colleagues still wore cloth masks, and now I was told it may be cancer and I'm peri-menopausal. Just hit me from all sides! So followed a few anxious weeks and then I went for a hysteroscopy at the hospital.

Much to my relief, someone somewhere had heard me and they were using forehead thermometers at the hospital entrance! Hooray! I was taken to speak to a consultant, and although she was lovely, I couldn't hear her very well.  They all still had cloth masks – no change there then.  A nurse talked very loudly telling me what I had to do. So,, I was trying to relax and not stress with my feet in stirrups, having taken both ibuprofen and paracetamol in anticipation of the pain, and then the consultant sat down in between my legs and started talking. I couldn't hear her, so the very helpful nurse stood by my side and talked very loudly repeating what the consultant had said. 'She says you're too tense, she can't get the speculum in the right place' 'You need to relax' 'Try and open your legs wider' Really? Honestly, I'm supposed to relax when it felt that the whole building could hear what the nurse was saying to me. The consultant finally gave up trying to get the polyp out but managed to take a small amount to do a biopsy. Then she could see me visibly wincing and booked me in for general anaesthetic. I couldn't get out of there fast enough! I didn't want to see who may have overheard in the adjoining cubicles. Sometimes you have to laugh! (By the way it was just a polyp and not cancerous so that was brilliant news.)

I had to go for my pre-op covid test today before the operation to remove the polyp. It was a drive through and I met the most wonderful woman. I explained I needed to lipread, and she popped into the office and came back out with a clear visor. She then made sure I could lipread and she also did some basic sign language that I understood. It really makes a stressful situation so much easier. I have a British Sign Language Stage 1 qualification but because I don't know anyone who uses sign

language I've not been able to practise, and
therefore I have forgotten most of it. A colleague at
work is keen to learn sign language so we will be
able to practise together which will be fantastic!

So the operation has taken place and it couldn't
have gone more smoothly. My blood pressure was
at an all-time high and my anxiety wasn't doing me
any favours, but from the moment I walked into
reception, the receptionist made everyone aware
that I needed to lipread. I must have spoken to 18
people that day and they all made the choice to
lower their masks, which was incredible. The
consultant, the anaesthetist and the surgeon all
made sure I knew exactly what was about to
happen. They said that taking out my hearing aids
and taking my glasses off would be the last thing I
would do before going under as I was worried I
would miss out on something. I had a surprise
when I came round; someone had put my hearing
aids back in for me so I could hear when I awoke
and my glasses were right next to me. They
couldn't have been nicer. Then when I was taken
to the recovery lounge, I spoke to a lovely lady who
had a hand crocheted extender at the back of her
mask so it didn't go behind her ears. I told her it
was a wonderful idea as the mask straps often hurt
my ears, what with having to deal with glasses and
hearing aids behind my ear as well. She
disappeared and came straight back with a lovely
deep red mask extender and gave it to me. I was so

touched. Anyway, the operation was a success which was a relief. Johnny and I are hoping it will be the last of our many hospital visits!
When it was time to leave, I was escorted back to the main reception area where Johnny was waiting with my chai latte from Costa. He knows me well!

## 29 **A NEW BEGINNING**
(November 2021)

It feels like we are coming out of covid and that there may be a light at the end of the tunnel. The GP has put me on medication which has really improved my mood and has lessened my menopausal symptoms, but I'll go back to talk through things further with her. I feel generally calmer about everything and my anxiety is under control for now. Johnny is much better now he has had the stoma reversal and I've had the operation. Onwards and upwards!

My way of dealing with face masks is to speak up, and more often than not people are usually fine with pulling down their mask – socially distanced of course. People may feel they are safe enough now not to worry about mask wearing. At work, I have my magic pen and we use clear masks on occasion. Of course, nothing compares to seeing someone's lips, but hopefully the end is in sight. A friend of my mums bought me a lanyard recently which says – 'I need to read your lips' which I quite like. I still don't feel ready to wear it yet, but maybe I will one day!

During Zoom calls and training sessions, the trainers are informed every time and I let them know at the start that I'm the one they have to make a fuss of! Not really but I feel I'm getting better at speaking up.

# I am deaf

Socially, I've realized that it is much better to see friends on a 1 to 1 basis.  That way we can have really good chats instead of me just sitting there trying to follow a conversation in a group and not being able to decipher what is being said.

Also, I think it's really good to talk! I like it when people ask about my hearing aids; it means that I can then explain my deafness and my needs. Obviously, I can't speak on behalf of all those who have some sort of hearing loss, this is just my personal experience and maybe not everyone will want to talk, but I think it would be a great start.

Also, to be deaf aware, please make sure you have the attention of the deaf person in front of you before you start speaking. Speak as you normally would. Speaking slowly just makes me feel upset and stupid. I remember getting really frustrated when I went to nightclubs with my friends and they always felt compelled to shout in my ear over the noise.  When I explained you could talk normally facing me, some of them found it really difficult not to keep shouting!

Remember not to cover your mouth when you speak, some people have nervous gestures  and keep doing that. This makes it more difficult for me to understand what you are saying.

# I am deaf

If we are having a movie night, we always put subtitles on. I'm convinced it helped the boys when they were younger with learning to read. The subtitles are invaluable to me, and it is really annoying when they are not available. I'm currently waiting to watch a documentary that has no subtitles available even though it says it does. Also, I've watched a tv series where subtitles are not available randomly during episode 5, but they are available for episodes 1 to 4 and 6. I literally have to miss an episode and as you can imagine, it drives me round the bend! Also, subtitles are known to be incorrect and rude when they're not supposed to be, which is quite funny sometimes, but I'd rather that than not have them at all.

At our church, we have a loop system fitted and a microphone. When people talk, they go to the front so I can see their faces. If I have issues, I have a wonderful friend who lip speaks for me so I lipread her instead of the person who is talking. It can make us both chuckle sometimes when she can't hear what is being said either!

If there is a group of us in a restaurant for example, I have a wonderful friend who always makes sure she talks directly at me when she is conversing with other people -it feels weird but it helps enormously!

Obviously, in places like a restaurant or somewhere

where we are going to be talking for a while, I always try to find out if the place has loud acoustics - I know which places I'm going to struggle in and which are going to allow me to enjoy a conversation.

I also want to make clear that my deafness is a part of me. Someone once asked if I wanted to be a hearing person and I said no. I've never been a hearing person so I don't miss it. Apparently I have a noise tolerance level so if I were to hear like my friends, it might be too loud for me. I like being able to switch off my hearing aids when I want to, to drive with no sound, to enjoy my friends and family's faces, lipreading the people on the other tables during quizzes (I'm sure that's not cheating...) and reading subtitles can make you chuckle sometimes. As I've said before, lipreading is my superpower; I am strong and unique and enough.

I was thinking the other day about the term – hard of hearing or hearing impaired. I've decided that for me personally, they have negative connotations. I've decided that for me, I'm most comfortable with the term – I am deaf.

I am deaf

Printed in Great Britain
by Amazon

70408790R00058